GREAT MASKS TO MAKE

Written by Robyn Supraner
Illustrated by Renzo Barto

Troll Associates

Library of Congress Cataloging in Publication Data

Supraner, Robyn.
    Great masks to make.

    SUMMARY: Includes instructions for easy-to-make
masks, including a wicked witch, chef, baboon, pirate,
and geisha.
        1. Masks—Juvenile literature.   [1. Masks.
2. Handicraft]   I. Barto, Renzo.   II. Title.
TT898.S96   731´.75   80-24077
ISBN 0-89375-436-6
ISBN 0-89375-437-4 (pbk.)

CONTENTS

BEFORE YOU BEGIN — Here are some hints that may help.

To Make a Cone:

1 Start with a circle. Use a compass or trace around a can, a coin, or a cup — anything round will do.

2 Cut out the circle. Make a slit from the edge of the circle to the center. Overlap the cut edges, and glue or tape them together. You will have a wide, flat cone.

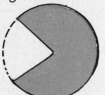 

3 For a taller cone, cut a pie-shaped wedge from the circle. The more you cut away, the taller and sharper the cone will be. Cones come in handy for making noses and horns on your masks.

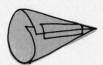 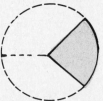

To Attach The Cone to Your Mask:

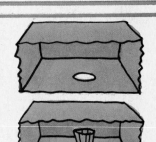

1 Cut a hole in the mask about the size of a half dollar.

2 Push the cone, point first, through the hole. Do not push the cone all the way through.

3 Make five or six slits in the wide end of the cone. Bend back the tabs, and glue or tape them to the inside of the mask.

For Sticking Things Together:

Use staples, tape, or glue. White glue is best for gluing paper.

4

To Curl Paper:

1 To make curly eyelashes, hair, and mustaches, cut wide or narrow strips of paper.

2 Curl the strips by wrapping them tightly around a pencil. For fat curls, use a thick pencil or the handle of a broom.

To Keep Your Mask in Place:

1 With a crayon, mark where the mask touches your ears.

2 Stick a loose-leaf reinforcement over each mark.

3 Poke a hole in the center of each reinforcement.

4 Attach strings or ribbons to the holes.

(*Note:* For lightweight paper, use reinforcements on both the front and back of your mask.)

Hint:

Have everything assembled *before* you begin. If you are missing something you need, try using something else. You may think of something even better!

Some Things To Do With Masks:

Write a play, and make a mask for each character. Act out the play yourself, by changing masks, or ask some friends to join the fun.

Make a mask of each member of your family. Have each person wear her or his own mask, then exchange masks and become the other person.

THE WICKED WITCH

Here's what you need:

Brown paper bag

Aluminum foil

Pencil

Colored construction paper

Thread or string

Scissors

Glue

Crayons

Tape

Marker pens

Loose-leaf reinforcements

Here's what you do:

1 Cut a large panel from the paper bag.

(*Note:* If there is writing on the outside of the bag, use the other side.)

2 Hold the paper to your face and, with a crayon, lightly mark where to cut holes for the eyes, nose, and mouth.

3 Cut two almond-shaped eyes. Cut a circle, about the size of a half dollar, for the nose. Cut an opening for the mouth. Make it wicked. Make it large enough to stick your tongue through!

4 From a sheet of black construction paper, cut out the witch's hair. Glue it in place. From the aluminum foil, make the crown. Turn the bottom edge under to make it straight and glue it in place above the hair.

5 Cut long, pointed eyelashes from black construction paper.

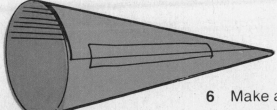

6 Make a long, pointed cone for the nose.

7 With a crayon, draw a fancy edge on the crown. Cut along the outline carefully. Also draw the witch's chin and cut the paper to shape the chin.

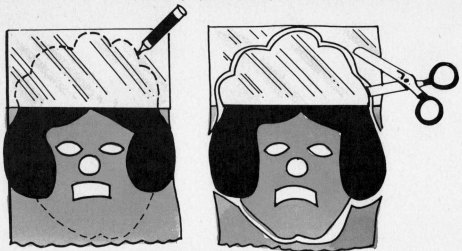

8 Glue the eyelashes in place. Fit the nose into the circle and tape it to the back of the mask.

9 Use a red marker to draw the witch's lips.

10 Add a beauty mark to the witch's chin.

11 Glue a loose-leaf reinforcement to each side of the back of the mask.

12 With a pencil, make a hole through the reinforcements. Tie a piece of string to each hole.

For a really *wicked* witch, make purple hair and a green mouth. Draw a strip of purple shadow above her eyes.

A smiling mouth and a smaller nose will give you a pleasant-looking queen mask. Put jewels on her crown. Cut them out from many different colors of construction paper.

THE KING

Here's what you need:

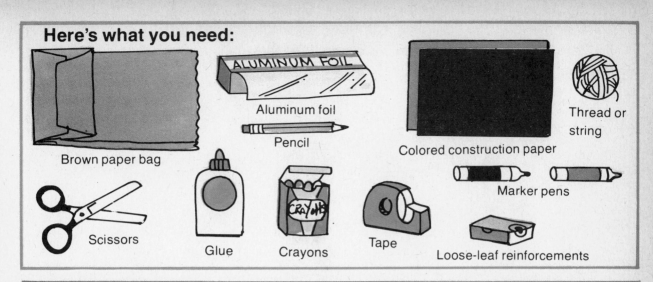

Brown paper bag

Aluminum foil

Pencil

Colored construction paper

Thread or string

Scissors

Glue

Crayons

Tape

Marker pens

Loose-leaf reinforcements

Here's what you do:

1 Cut a large panel from the paper bag.

2 Hold the paper to your face and, with a crayon, lightly mark where to cut holes for the eyes, nose, and mouth.

3 Cut two triangles for the eyes. Cut a long triangle for the nose. Cut a rectangle for the mouth.

4 On another piece of the paper bag, cut out the pattern for the king's nose. Fold along the dotted lines.

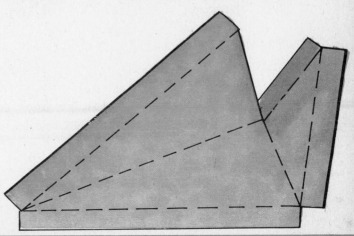

5 Glue the flap. Fit the nose in place, and tape the tabs to the back of the mask.

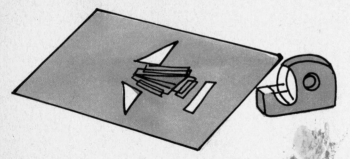 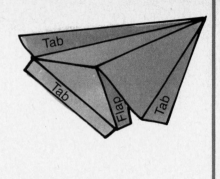

6 Turn the mask over. Using a black marker, outline the eyes and draw the eyebrows. Use a red marker to outline the mouth.

7 Cut out a hat shape from red paper.

8 From black paper, cut out the hair, mustache, and beard.

9 Use aluminum foil to make the crown. Fold one edge of the foil under to make a straight edge. Cut the other edge of the foil so that the crown has three points.

10   Glue the hat in place. Glue the hair below the hat.

11   Glue the crown in place. Cut away the extra brown paper above the hat. Draw the shape of the face and chin. Then trim away the brown paper along the face outline.

12   Glue the mustache and beard in place.

13   Glue a loose-leaf reinforcement to each side of the mask. Poke a hole in the center of the reinforcements and tie a piece of string through each hole.

If you like, try making a curly mustache or beard. You can also change the expression on the king's face by changing the shape of his eyebrows.

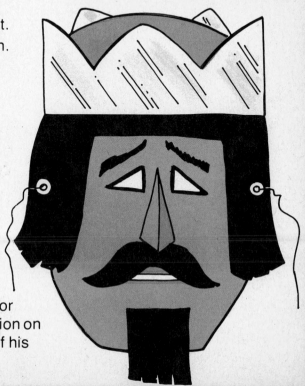

THE KNIGHT

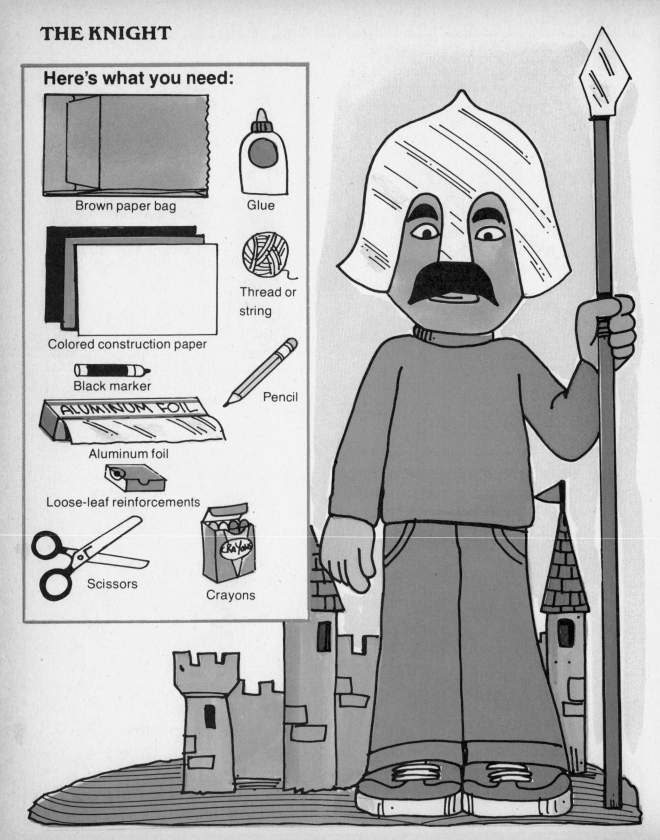

Here's what you need:

Brown paper bag

Glue

Colored construction paper

Thread or string

Black marker

Pencil

ALUMINUM FOIL

Aluminum foil

Loose-leaf reinforcements

Scissors

CRaYons

Crayons

Here's what you do:

1 Cut a large panel from a paper bag.

2 Hold the paper to your face and, with a crayon, lightly mark where to cut holes for the eyes and mouth.

3 Cut two almond-shaped eyes. Cut a rectangle for the mouth.

4 From black construction paper, cut eyebrows and a long, droopy mustache. Glue them in place on your mask.

5 Copy the pattern for the knight's helmet onto aluminum foil. Very carefully, cut it out and glue it in place.

6 With a black marker, outline the eyes and lower lip.

7 Cut away the bottom of the mask to make a chin.

8 Cut away the top of the mask to fit the shape of the helmet.

9 Add loose-leaf reinforcements and string, as done with the other masks.

THE DRAGON

Here's what you need:

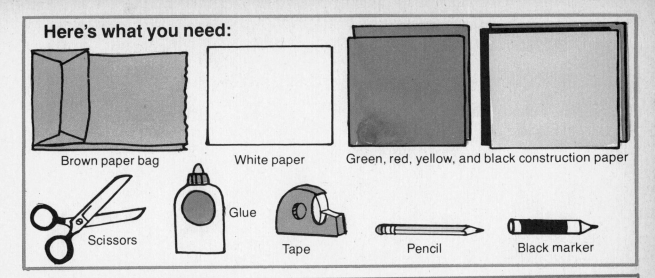

Brown paper bag

White paper

Green, red, yellow, and black construction paper

Scissors

Glue

Tape

Pencil

Black marker

Here's what you do:

1 Put the paper bag on your head, and lightly mark where to cut holes for the eyes and mouth.

2 Cut two almond-shaped eyes. Outline the eyes with black marker.

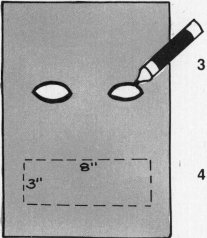

8"

3"

3 From red construction paper, cut out a rectangle to fit in the dotted area shown at left. Glue the red rectangle to the paper bag.

4 From white paper, cut out about fifteen small triangles. Make them about the size shown at right. These are the dragon's teeth.

5 Glue the teeth in place. Outline the mouth and each tooth with black marker.

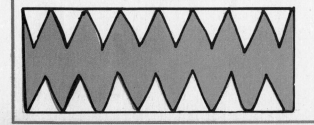

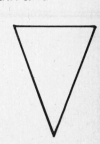

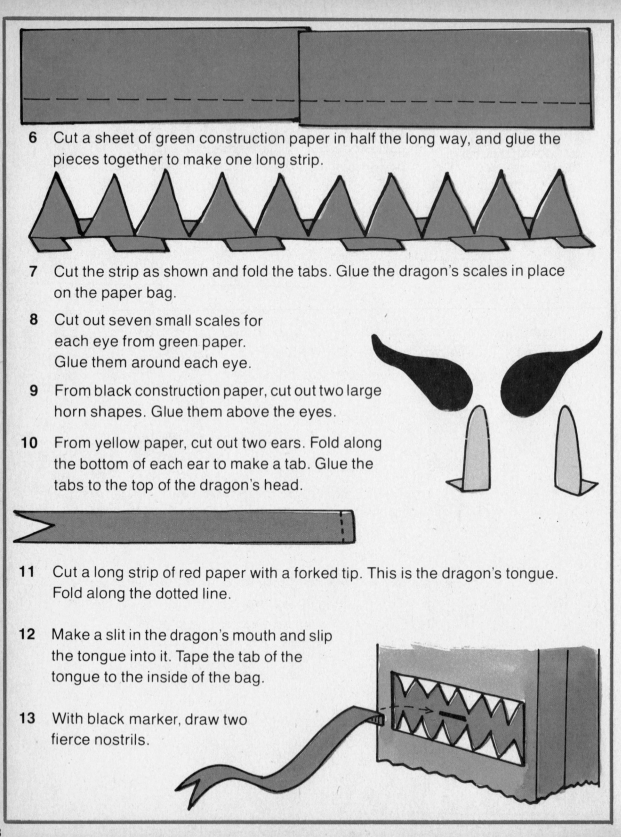

6 Cut a sheet of green construction paper in half the long way, and glue the pieces together to make one long strip.

7 Cut the strip as shown and fold the tabs. Glue the dragon's scales in place on the paper bag.

8 Cut out seven small scales for each eye from green paper. Glue them around each eye.

9 From black construction paper, cut out two large horn shapes. Glue them above the eyes.

10 From yellow paper, cut out two ears. Fold along the bottom of each ear to make a tab. Glue the tabs to the top of the dragon's head.

11 Cut a long strip of red paper with a forked tip. This is the dragon's tongue. Fold along the dotted line.

12 Make a slit in the dragon's mouth and slip the tongue into it. Tape the tab of the tongue to the inside of the bag.

13 With black marker, draw two fierce nostrils.

THE PRINCESS

Here's what you need:

Colored construction paper

Scissors

Aluminum foil

Pencil

Crayon

Black and pink markers

Tape

Glue

Here's what you do:

1. Hold a sheet of pink construction paper up to your face. With a crayon, lightly mark where to cut holes for the eyes, nose, and mouth.

2. Cut two almond-shaped eyes. Cut a circle, about the size of a half dollar, for the nose. Cut a half-moon shape for the mouth.

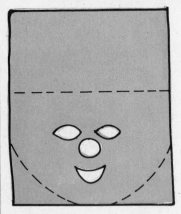

3. Fold one edge of a sheet of aluminum foil to make a straight edge. Glue the strip of foil to the pink paper.

4. Cut points in the foil to make the crown.

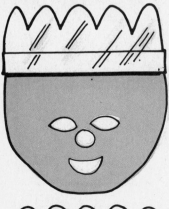

5. On a sheet of black construction paper, copy this pattern for the eyelashes. Cut and curl the lashes. Glue them in place.

6. Draw a fringe of black eyelashes under the eyes.

7. Outline the mouth, using pink marker. Draw two pink cheeks.

8. Make a small cone for her nose. Tape it in place to the back of the mask.

9. Make fat curls from yellow construction paper. Glue them to the sides of the face. Glue some hair to her forehead, too.

10. Shape the bottom of the mask to make a chin.

11. Draw a beauty mark and thin eyebrows.

THE CHEF

Here's what you need:

Pencil

Red and pink crayons

Black marker

Scissors

Colored construction paper

Oak tag

Glue

Here's what you do:

1 Hold a sheet of construction paper up to your face. Any color will do. With a crayon, lightly mark where to cut holes for the eyes and mouth.

2 Cut two circles for the eyes. Cut a rectangle for the mouth.

3 From a sheet of black paper, cut a fringe of curly hair and a big mustache. Glue them in place.

4 On a light-colored sheet of paper, copy the pattern for the chef's hat. Cut it out and glue it to the mask.

 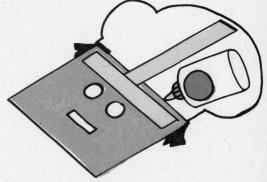

5 Cut two strips of oak tag. Glue them in place behind the mask, as shown. This will keep the chef's hat from falling over.

6 Decorate the mask. Cut away the paper to make a chin. Draw a round, cherry nose and two red cheeks. Draw eyelashes and outline all the features of the face in black. Glue a triangle of black paper to the chin for a beard.

THE RABBIT

Here's what you need:

Colored construction paper

Oak tag

Scissors

Pencil

Crayon

Black and blue markers

Glue

24

Here's what you do:

1   Hold a sheet of oak tag up to your face. With a crayon, lightly mark where to cut holes for the eyes.

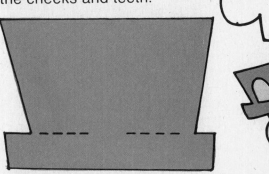

2   Cut two circles for the eyes. Draw the outline of the face and cut it out.

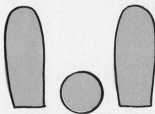

3   From pink construction paper, cut out two smaller ears and a circle for the nose. From white paper, cut out this shape for the cheeks and teeth.

4   On a sheet of construction paper, copy the hat pattern. Make two slits along the dotted lines. Cut out the hat. Slip the ears through the slits and glue in place.

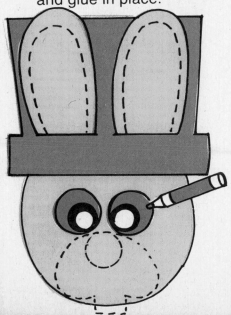

5   Using blue marker, draw large blue circles around the eyes.

6   Glue cheeks, teeth, nose, and ears in place.

7   Using black marker, outline cheeks, teeth, eyes, and nose. Draw three whiskers on each cheek.

Can you change this mask around a bit and make it a puppy? A kitten? What other animals can you make?

THE FUNNY POLICE OFFICER

Here's what you need:

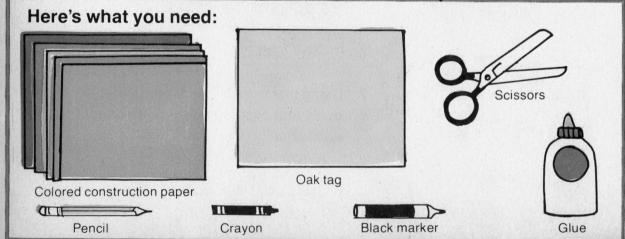

Colored construction paper

Oak tag

Scissors

Glue

Pencil

Crayon

Black marker

Here's what you do:

1. Hold a sheet of construction paper up to your face. With crayon, lightly mark where to cut holes for the eyes and mouth.

2. Cut two round holes for the eyes and a rectangle for the mouth.

3. Cut two circles for cheeks from orange construction paper. Cut out a larger circle from red paper for the nose. Glue everything in place.

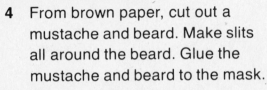

4. From brown paper, cut out a mustache and beard. Make slits all around the beard. Glue the mustache and beard to the mask.

5. From blue construction paper, cut out the hat. Glue it to the face. Cut a star out of yellow paper and glue it to the hat. With black marker, draw details on the hat and star.

(*Note:* To strengthen the hat, add oak-tag strips behind the mask, as was done for the Chef Mask on page 22.)

BOX MASKS

Here's what you need:

Empty cereal boxes

Colored construction paper

Scissors

Black marker

Pencil

Ruler

Glue

Here's what you do:

1   Cut the back and bottom panels off an empty cereal box.

2   Cover the box with construction paper. Measure the sides or trace around them, so the paper cover will fit. Use a ruler to make the lines straight.

3   Cut out eyeglasses from blue construction paper.

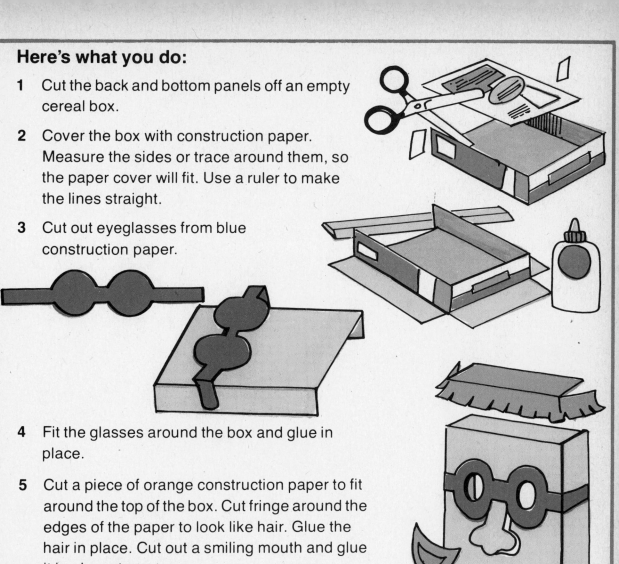

4   Fit the glasses around the box and glue in place.

5   Cut a piece of orange construction paper to fit around the top of the box. Cut fringe around the edges of the paper to look like hair. Glue the hair in place. Cut out a smiling mouth and glue it in place, too.

6   Cut two circles through the glasses and the box for the eyes.

7   Cut out a flap from the box for a nose.

8   Outline the nose and mouth with black marker. Add eyebrows.

9   Decorate cereal-box masks any way you like. Try pipe cleaners for whiskers. Clumps of cotton, heavy yarn, and crumpled tissue paper make good hair, beards, and mustaches. Make hats and horns with paper cups. Use sequins and glitter and toothpicks. Use sponges and seashells and leaves. A bit of glue and some imagination are all you need! On the following pages are some ideas you might like to try.

THE BABOON

To make a baboon mask, cut away only part of the back panel of the cereal box. Fold out the two flaps to make ears.

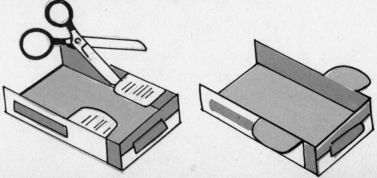

THE WALRUS

1   Make two tusks out of oak tag. Glue them in place under cotton whiskers.

2   For a monocle, bend a pipe cleaner into a circle. Tie some string to the pipe cleaner, and glue in place.

THE ROBOT

1 Cut the bottom off an empty cereal box, so you have a small strip.

2 Cover the small strip with aluminum foil and glue it to the top of the large part of the box.

3 Glue more foil to a strip of oak tag. Cut it out and glue it to the lower part of the mask. Add circles cut from construction paper to the front and sides of the mask. Add colored panels for eyes and mouth. Outline them with black marker. Cut out two small holes for the eyes.

Here's what you need:

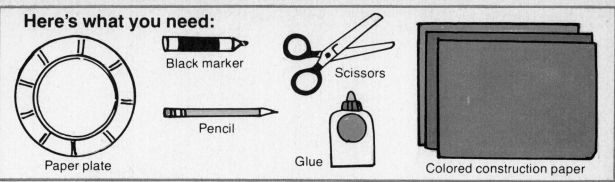

Paper plate

Black marker

Pencil

Scissors

Glue

Colored construction paper

Here's what you do:

1 Hold a paper plate up to your face. Lightly mark where to cut holes for the eyes and mouth.

2 Cut two half-moon shapes for the eyes. Cut a rectangle for the mouth.

3 With black marker, draw a nose, and outline the eyes and mouth.

4 Cut hair and braids from black construction paper. Glue them in place to the plate.

5 Cut two strips of another color paper. Glue them to the braids.

6 Make a pretty headband. Glue over the hair.

7 Add a fancy feather.

8 Cut out red circles for cheeks and glue in place.

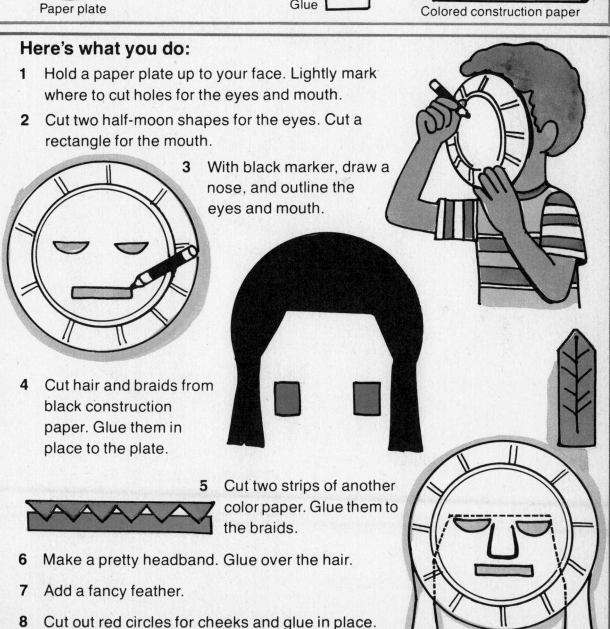

THE PIRATE

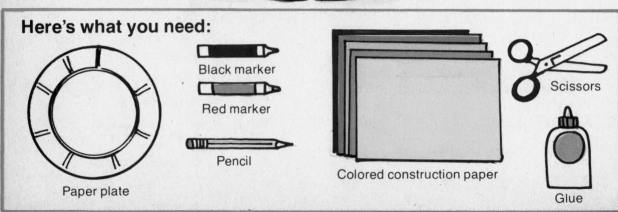

36

Here's what you do:

1 Hold a paper plate up to your face, and lightly mark where to cut holes for the eyes and mouth.

2 Cut two almond-shaped eyes. Cut out a smiling mouth that has one tooth.

3 With black marker, draw in a nose and outline the eyes. Using red marker, outline the mouth.

4 Make the pirate's beard by gluing strips of dark blue construction paper around the edge of the mask. Curl the beard by wrapping the strips of paper around a pencil.

5 For a colorful bandana, cut a sheet of red construction paper as shown. Cut out circles from yellow paper. Glue them to the bandana. Then glue the bandana to the mask.

6 Cut two circles from orange paper and glue in place for the cheeks.

7 Cut out an eye patch and glue it in place.

THE GEISHA

Here's what you need:

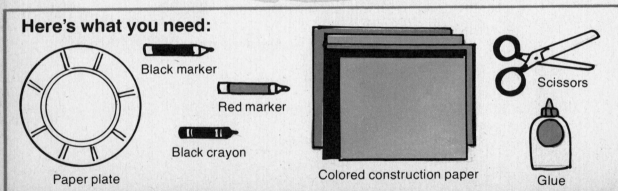

Paper plate

Black marker

Red marker

Black crayon

Colored construction paper

Scissors

Glue

Here's what you do:

1 Hold a paper plate up to your face, and with crayon, lightly mark where to cut holes for the eyes.

2 Cut two small circles for the eyes.

3 With black marker, outline the eyes. Draw eyebrows and two nostrils.

4 Using red marker, draw heart-shaped lips.

5 Cut two circles from orange construction paper for cheeks. Glue them to the mask.

6 From black paper, cut out the shape of the hair. Make two small slits on each side of the hair, near the bottom.

7 Slip the plate into the hair and glue in place.

8 From purple paper, cut two eyelids and glue to face.

9 Cut two pink flowers and several green leaves. Glue them to the geisha's hair.

THE CAT

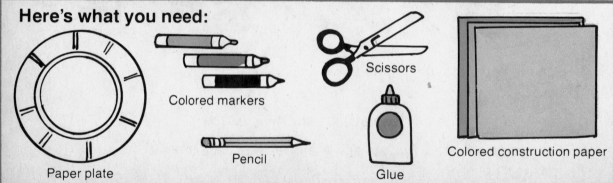

Here's what you need:

Paper plate

Colored markers

Pencil

Scissors

Glue

Colored construction paper

40

Here's what you do:

1 Hold a paper plate up to your face, and lightly mark where the eyes and mouth will go.

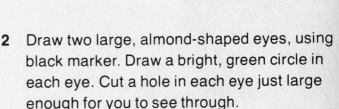

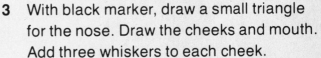

2 Draw two large, almond-shaped eyes, using black marker. Draw a bright, green circle in each eye. Cut a hole in each eye just large enough for you to see through.

3 With black marker, draw a small triangle for the nose. Draw the cheeks and mouth. Add three whiskers to each cheek.

4 Cut away the lower part of the plate, as shown here. Carefully, cut around the whiskers.

5 Color the nose pink. Make the cheeks light brown. Make the mouth red.

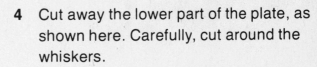

6 Cut two ears out of brown paper.

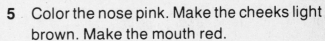

7 Cut two smaller ears out of pink paper, and glue them to the brown ears. Then glue the brown ears to the back of the mask.

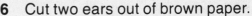

8 With black marker, draw a few whiskers on the cat's forehead.

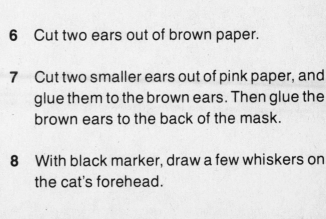

THE OWL

Here's what you need:

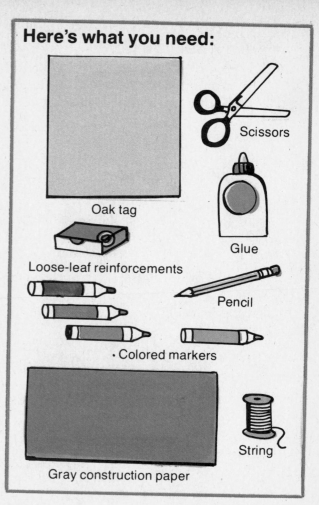

Oak tag

Scissors

Loose-leaf reinforcements

Glue

Pencil

· Colored markers

String

Gray construction paper

Here's what you do:

1 Draw this shape on gray construction paper. Make slits across the top, as shown.

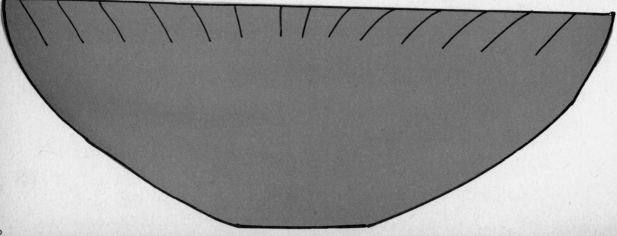

2 Using this picture to guide you, draw the owl's face on oak tag. Color it with your markers. Outline everything in black.

3 Cut out the mask.

4 Slightly curl the sides of the mask with a pencil.

5 Glue the gray feathers above the eyes.

6 Cut out two half circles outlined by the dotted areas in the eyes. Make a small hole near each edge of the mask. Stick a loose-leaf reinforcement around each hole.

7 Tie a string through each hole, and tie the mask around your head.

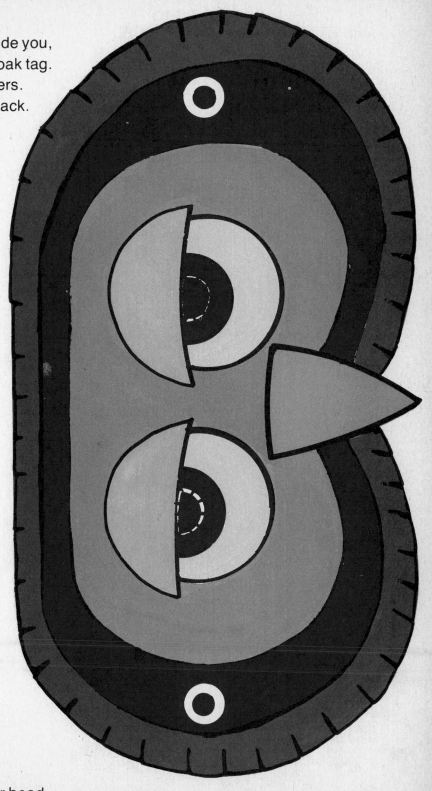

PAPIER-MÂCHÉ MASKS

Here's what you need:

Spoon

Scissors

Balloon

Water

Flour

Bowl

String

Poster paints and brush

Black marker

Newspapers

Here's what you do:

1 Using black marker, draw outlines for the eyes and mouth of the mask on an inflated balloon. (Because you will only cover half of the balloon with papier-mâché, keep the face on one half of the balloon.)

2 Mix flour and water in a bowl. Stir until the flour is completely dissolved. Let the mixture thicken.

3 Tear single sheets of newspaper into strips that are about one to two inches wide. The strips can be ragged. Rip enough strips to cover half of the balloon a few times.

4 Dip the strips of paper, one at a time, into the flour. Squeeze off the extra paste.

5 Place the strips of paper over the balloon. Do not cover the areas you marked for the eyes and mouth. Cover only half of the balloon.

6 After one layer of newspaper dries, add another layer. Then add another layer.

45

7 After about two days, when the papier-mâché mask has completely dried, pop the balloon.

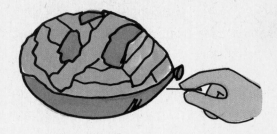

8 Use scissors to trim around the edge of the mask and around the openings for the eyes and mouth.

9 Use poster paints to decorate the mask. Here are some designs you can use. Or create some of your own!

10 When the paint has dried, make two small holes at either side of the mask. Tie a string through each hole.

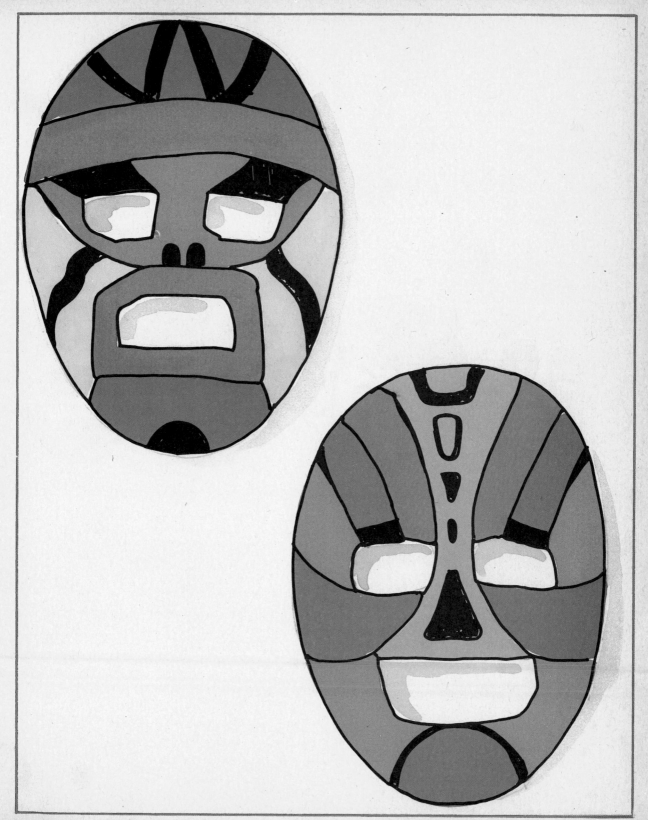